Three King Mage's Magick

S ROB

DEDICATION

I dedicate this book to my mother and father.

CONTENTS

ACKNOWLEDGMENTS

I acknowledge the existence of real magick

Chapter 1 Protection

The magick in this book draws on the power of three very well known and important historical biblical figures and these are the three wisemen, they could and should be described as Kings, astrologers and mages: occultists all. It was these three figures that travelled to the correct location and time to meet Jesus: a figure many call Our Lord, he who is gods son and god himself: the one and only Christian god. The three wise men were so good at astrology and astronomy: as it existed then as one subject: that they were able too travel to Jesus as he was being born and gave him three gifts gold: a precious metal: frankincense a substance used in perfumes and incense: and also myrrh: an a sweet smelling resin. It should be noted that these were all highly expensive gifts. But we do not work magick to summon he they showed homage to: Jesus: but they themselves. These figures named Balthazar, Gaspar and Melchior where part of an occult or priestly class. We will use these figures together and it is this way because they acted together, they arrived at the same destination and time and this way shall it be for all time.

But to summon then we shall be using the help of the Roman god Janus: who has two faces. It is in fact the case that with one face Janus sees the future and with the other the past. Janus is a god who control doorways and yes, I am using the word god to relate to Janus as well as the Christian god and this is because within both of their frameworks, they are both gods. In fact, because Janus control doorways he can open a doorway so that the three King Mages: three wise men: can come through to our world. We will then ask for what we want and they shall depart from our world back through the doorway and we shall get Janus to shut the doorway again. However, there is no natural limits to what we may ask these three King Mages for: these three Wise Men may be asked for anything at all. I therefore think that with this in mind we should start off with protection because protection is a sort of magick we can work even when we do not actually want anything at all: it also is good to simply practice the technique of working magick. But it should always be the case that the fuel for the magick is your human will. Will is a strong force and this along with intent: that you intend magick to be worked: is what gets the three King Mages to do as you desire. I think the best way to get started is to work some magick and here it is.

Three King Mages magick for protection

Janus the powerful Roman god, he with two faces and while one looks towards the future another looks towards the past. Janus you control doorways and so I ask that you open the doorway that leads to the Three King Mages, the men of wisdom, Balthazar, Gaspar and Melchior, they who brought the three presents of gold, frankincense and myrrh. Janus open the doorway: Janus does open the doorway it is opening it is open here and now. I summon through the doorway the King Mage Balthazar, he who carried gold. Balthazar, King Mage step through the doorway and be here with me: Balthazar does step

3

through the doorway and is here with me. King Mage Gaspar you who carried the gift of frankincense, I ask that you come through the doorway and be here with me, Gaspar the wise man, I ask that you come to this place: Gaspar does step through the doorway and is here with me. King Mage Melchior he who carried myrrh, I ask that you step through the doorway and be here with me: Melchior does step through the doorway and is here with me. Balthazar, I ask that you protect me from all harm from all attacks no matter what the source. Gaspar, I ask that you protect me from all attacks and all harm no matter what the source. Melchior, I ask that you protect me from any and all attacks, protect me from all harm. Balthazar agrees to help and departs back through the doorway. Gaspar agrees to help and departs back through the doorway. Melchior agrees to help and departs back through the doorway. Janus the powerful Roman god, he with two faces and while one looks towards the future another looks towards the past. Janus you control doorways and so I ask that you shut the

4

doorway, Janus close the doorway: Janus does shut the doorway it is closing it is closed here and now. So it is and will be.

I feel I should share with you that even simply typing this ritual you have just performed into the computer caused at least one of the three Kings to appear: Balthazar. You should therefore expect no less when you perform the other magick from this book. This magick is potent and powerful. This next magick is to protect the area you are in and so this magick is best performed at home.

Three King Mages magick to protect a place

Janus the powerful Roman god, he with two faces and while one looks towards the future another looks towards the past. Janus you control doorways and so I ask that you open the doorway that leads to the Three King Mages, the men of wisdom, Balthazar, Gaspar and Melchior, they who brought the three presents of gold, frankincense and myrrh. Janus open the doorway: Janus does open the doorway it is opening it is open here and now. I summon through the doorway

5

the King Mage Balthazar, he who carried gold. Balthazar, King Mage step through the doorway and be here with me: Balthazar does step through the doorway and is here with me. King Mage Gaspar you who carried the gift of frankincense, I ask that you come through the doorway and be here with me, Gaspar the wise man, I ask that you come to this place: Gaspar does step through the doorway and is here with me. King Mage Melchior he who carried myrrh, I ask that you step through the doorway and be here with me: Melchior does step through the doorway and is here with me. Balthazar, I ask that you protect this place and all around and within it from all harm from all attacks no matter what the source. Gaspar, I ask that you protect this place and all around and within it from all attacks and all harm no matter what the source. Melchior, I ask that you protect this place and all around and within it from any and all attacks, from all harm. Balthazar agrees to help and departs back through the doorway. Gaspar agrees to help and departs back through the doorway. Melchior agrees to help and departs back through the doorway. Janus

6

the powerful Roman god, he with two faces and while one looks

towards the future another looks towards the past. Janus you control

doorways and so I ask that you shut the doorway, Janus close the

doorway: Janus does shut the doorway it is closing it is closed here

and now. So it is and will be.

This magick that follows is for you to protect someone of your own

choosing. This means that this magick can protect a friend, family, or

anyone at all. However, it is easiest if this magick is done to protect

someone you know at least quite well. Will this magick to work and it

shall.

Three King Mages magick to protect a chosen person

Janus the powerful Roman god, he with two faces and while one

looks towards the future another looks towards the past. Janus you

control doorways and so I ask that you open the doorway that leads

to the Three King Mages, the men of wisdom, Balthazar, Gaspar and

Melchior, they who brought the three presents of gold, frankincense and myrrh. Janus open the doorway: Janus does open the doorway it

is opening it is open here and now. I summon through the doorway

the King Mage Balthazar, he who carried gold. Balthazar, King Mage

step through the doorway and be here with me: Balthazar does step

through the doorway and is here with me. King Mage Gaspar you

who carried the gift of frankincense, I ask that you come through the

doorway and be here with me, Gaspar the wise man, I ask that you

come to this place: Gaspar does step through the doorway and is here

with me. King Mage Melchior he who carried myrrh, I ask that you

step through the doorway and be here with me: Melchior does step

through the doorway and is here with me. Balthazar, I ask that you

protect <u>state name of chosen person</u> from all harm from all attacks no

matter what the source. Gaspar, I ask that you protect <u>state name of</u>

<u>chosen person</u> from all attacks and all harm no matter what the

source. Melchior, I ask that you protect <u>state name of chosen person</u>

from any and all attacks, protect them from all harm. Balthazar agrees

to help and departs back through the doorway. Gaspar agrees to help

8

and departs back through the doorway. Melchior agrees to help and departs back through the doorway. Janus the powerful Roman god, he with two faces and while one looks towards the future another looks towards the past. Janus you control doorways and so I ask that you shut the doorway, Janus close the doorway: Janus does shut the doorway it is closing it is closed here and now. So it is and will be.

You have now worked magick from this the first chapter: and if you haven't you should choose at least one spell before you proceed. This isn't practical magick and so working all that is here is perfectly feasible: but do try some at least. You have gained in knowledge and you will gain more as you proceed.

Chapter 2 Good luck

I will now show you some magick for general good luck: that multipurpose sort of good luck which helps us with everything, the great facilitator of all that we do helping us to be a success. However, do not think you must pick a type of good luck because you can try all of the magick in this chapter; will this magick to work and it shall.

Three King Mages magick for general good luck

Janus the powerful Roman god, he with two faces and while one looks towards the future another looks towards the past. Janus you control doorways and so I ask that you open the doorway that leads to the Three King Mages, the men of wisdom, Balthazar, Gaspar and Melchior, they who brought the three presents of gold, frankincense and myrrh. Janus open the doorway: Janus does open the doorway it is opening it is open here and now. I summon through the doorway the King Mage Balthazar, he who carried gold. Balthazar, King Mage

step through the doorway and be here with me: Balthazar does step through the doorway and is here with me. King Mage Gaspar you who carried the gift of frankincense, I ask that you come through the doorway and be here with me, Gaspar the wise man, I ask that you come to this place: Gaspar does step through the doorway and is here with me. King Mage Melchior he who carried myrrh, I ask that you step through the doorway and be here with me: Melchior does step through the doorway and is here with me. Balthazar, I ask that you give me the gift of good luck. Gaspar, I ask that you give me the gift of good luck. Melchior, I ask that you give me the gift of good luck. Balthazar agrees to help and departs back through the doorway. Gaspar agrees to help and departs back through the doorway. Melchior agrees to help and departs back through the doorway. Janus the powerful Roman god, he with two faces and while one looks towards the future another looks towards the past. Janus you control doorways and so I ask that you shut the doorway, Janus close the doorway: Janus does shut the doorway it is closing it is closed here and now. So it is and will be.

There is a special focused sort of luck that helps us win at gambling and all games of chance. However, this good luck isn't necessarily enough always, it helps you win but rarely does so every time. But good luck at gambling is enough to make you rich and so change your life.

Three King Mages magick for gambling good luck

Janus the powerful Roman god, he with two faces and while one looks towards the future another looks towards the past. Janus you control doorways and so I ask that you open the doorway that leads to the Three King Mages, the men of wisdom, Balthazar, Gaspar and Melchior, they who brought the three presents of gold, frankincense and myrrh. Janus open the doorway: Janus does open the doorway it is opening it is open here and now. I summon through the doorway the King Mage Balthazar, he who carried gold. Balthazar, King Mage

12

step through the doorway and be here with me: Balthazar does step

through the doorway and is here with me. King Mage Gaspar you

who carried the gift of frankincense, I ask that you come through the

doorway and be here with me, Gaspar the wise man, I ask that you

come to this place: Gaspar does step through the doorway and is here

with me. King Mage Melchior he who carried myrrh, I ask that you

step through the doorway and be here with me: Melchior does step

through the doorway and is here with me. Balthazar, I ask that you

give me the gift of gambling good luck. Gaspar, I ask that you give

me the gift of gambling good luck. Melchior, I ask that you give me

the gift of gambling good luck. Balthazar agrees to help and departs

back through the doorway. Gaspar agrees to help and departs back

through the doorway. Melchior agrees to help and departs back

through the doorway. Janus the powerful Roman god, he with two

faces and while one looks towards the future another looks towards

the past. Janus you control doorways and so I ask that you shut the doorway, Janus close the doorway: Janus does shut the doorway it is

closing it is closed here and now. So it is and will be.

I now offer magick for good fortune and this is a little different from

good luck because it is good luck of the things which make our life

comfortable; opulent even. I think we all need this; we all wish to live

as good a life as we can and what comes next will assist you to do just

that.

Three King Mages magick for good fortune

Janus the powerful Roman god, he with two faces and while one

looks towards the future another looks towards the past. Janus you

control doorways and so I ask that you open the doorway that leads

to the Three King Mages, the men of wisdom, Balthazar, Gaspar and

Melchior, they who brought the three presents of gold, frankincense

and myrrh. Janus open the doorway: Janus does open the doorway it

is opening it is open here and now. I summon through the doorway

the King Mage Balthazar, he who carried gold. Balthazar, King Mage step through the doorway and be here with me: Balthazar does step through the doorway and is here with me. King Mage Gaspar you who carried the gift of frankincense, I ask that you come through the doorway and be here with me, Gaspar the wise man, I ask that you come to this place: Gaspar does step through the doorway and is here with me. King Mage Melchior he who carried myrrh, I ask that you step through the doorway and be here with me: Melchior does step through the doorway and is here with me. Balthazar, I ask that you give me the gift of good fortune. Gaspar, I ask that you give me the gift of good fortune. Melchior, I ask that you give me the gift of good fortune. Balthazar agrees to help and departs back through the doorway. Gaspar agrees to help and departs back through the doorway. Melchior agrees to help and departs back through the doorway. Janus the powerful Roman god, he with two faces and while one looks towards the future another looks towards the past. Janus you control doorways and so I ask that you shut the doorway, Janus close the doorway: Janus does shut the doorway it is closing it is closed here and now. So it is and will be.

You have learnt how to work even more magick and has expanded the range of experiences you have had because you had not performed this magick because the knowledge exists only within this book. However, this magick is a good servant and one good servant: or three in the guise of three wise men: is enough if he is clever enough to help you change your life. But do not think that whatever magick you work that you only pay some small part within it. In fact, you are central to this magick and your life: so please do not use only magical assistance to improve your life also use your mundane non-magical efforts too. By coupling your magick with your non-magical actions you will discover that achieving the goals you desire will be made very much easier.

Chapter 3 Power

Power is what stops us from being enslaved and to be a slave is a most piteous state to be in: yes, slavery exists still. In many ways the way of occultism is the pursuit of power and yet it also provides us enlightenment because many occultists are in many ways more of the mind than the body and yet they come to realise that thought and the physical are in reality, linked and many times can be one. The magick you will learn next is for greater power. I want to point out that this next magick is for power generally it isn't for any one type of power, just for greater power: and here it is.

Three King Mages magick for greater power

Janus the powerful Roman god, he with two faces and while one looks towards the future another looks towards the past. Janus you control doorways and so I ask that you open the doorway that leads to the Three King Mages, the men of wisdom, Balthazar, Gaspar and

Melchior, they who brought the three presents of gold, frankincense and myrrh. Janus open the doorway: Janus does open the doorway it is opening it is open here and now. I summon through the doorway the King Mage Balthazar, he who carried gold. Balthazar, King Mage step through the doorway and be here with me: Balthazar does step through the doorway and is here with me. King Mage Gaspar you who carried the gift of frankincense, I ask that you come through the doorway and be here with me, Gaspar the wise man, I ask that you come to this place: Gaspar does step through the doorway and is here with me. King Mage Melchior he who carried myrrh, I ask that you step through the doorway and be here with me: Melchior does step through the doorway and is here with me. Balthazar, I ask that you give me greater power. Gaspar, I ask that you give me greater power. Melchior, I ask that you give me greater power. Balthazar agrees to help and departs back through the doorway. Gaspar agrees to help and departs back through the doorway. Melchior agrees to help and departs back through the doorway. Janus the powerful Roman god, he with two faces and while one looks towards the future another looks towards the past. Janus you control doorways and so I ask that you shut the doorway, Janus close the doorway: Janus does shut the doorway it is closing it is closed here and now. So it is and will be.

Sometimes the only power that is needed is power over other people. I understand that to some people this is what social class is, it is how many people tell you what to do and how many people do you tell what to do. Power over people may not be as easy to assess as money but from it flows many great things and the world could be yours with this power.

Three King Mages magick for power over other people

Janus the powerful Roman god, he with two faces and while one looks towards the future another looks towards the past. Janus you control doorways and so I ask that you open the doorway that leads to the Three King Mages, the men of wisdom, Balthazar, Gaspar and Melchior, they who brought the three presents of gold, frankincense and myrrh. Janus open the doorway: Janus does open the doorway it is opening it is open here and now. I summon through the doorway the King Mage Balthazar, he who carried gold. Balthazar, King Mage step through the doorway and be here with me: Balthazar does step through the doorway and is here with me. King Mage Gaspar you who carried the gift of frankincense, I ask that you come through the doorway and be here with me, Gaspar the wise man, I ask that you come to this place: Gaspar does step through the doorway and is here with me. King Mage Melchior he who carried myrrh, I ask that you step through the doorway and be here with me: Melchior does step through the doorway and is here with me. Balthazar, I ask that you give me greater power over other people. Gaspar, I ask that you give me greater power over other people. Melchior, I ask that you give me greater power over other people. Balthazar agrees to help and departs back through the doorway. Gaspar agrees to help and departs back through the doorway. Melchior agrees to help and departs back through the doorway. Janus the powerful Roman god, he with two faces and while one looks towards the future another looks towards the past. Janus you control doorways and so I ask that you shut the doorway, Janus close the doorway: Janus does shut the doorway it is closing it is closed here and now. So it is and will be.

There are times when the power we need is power over an organization. However, this will likely as not also require some sort of mundane non-magical actions also. But controlling an organization can give us immense power. However, power isn't that useful unless we know what to do with it. However, to work this next magick you will need the name of the organization you want more power over; magick follows.

Three King Mages magick for power over a chosen organization

Janus the powerful Roman god, he with two faces and while one looks towards the future another looks towards the past. Janus you control doorways and so I ask that you open the doorway that leads to the Three King Mages, the men of wisdom, Balthazar, Gaspar and

Melchior, they who brought the three presents of gold, frankincense and myrrh. Janus open the doorway: Janus does open the doorway it is opening it is open here and now. I summon through the doorway the King Mage Balthazar, he who carried gold. Balthazar, King Mage step through the doorway and be here with me: Balthazar does step through the doorway and is here with me. King Mage Gaspar you who carried the gift of frankincense, I ask that you come through the doorway and be here with me, Gaspar the wise man, I ask that you come to this place: Gaspar does step through the doorway and is here with me. King Mage Melchior he who carried myrrh, I ask that you step through the doorway and be here with me: Melchior does step through the doorway and is here with me. Balthazar, I ask that you give me greater power over the organization named <u>state name of chosen organization</u>. Gaspar, I ask that you give me greater power over the organization named <u>state name of chosen organization</u>. Melchior, I ask that you give me greater power over the organization named <u>state name of chosen organization</u>. Balthazar agrees to help and departs back through the doorway. Gaspar agrees to help and departs back through the doorway. Melchior agrees to help and departs back through the doorway. Janus the powerful Roman god, he with two faces and while one looks towards the future another looks towards the past. Janus you control doorways and so I ask that you shut the doorway, Janus close the doorway: Janus does shut the doorway it is closing it is closed here and now. So it is and will be.

I feel that you should know that when first working magick that we usually have to make a few mistakes in order to progress but here you don't. In fact, here the magick is very much fool proofed it is made in such a way that there is nothing to go wrong. But you can still advance by altering the occasional word of the spells and see what happens when you do. In fact, I feel this is most beneficial. But please do realise that magick works best when it is used with a strong will and with you using that same strong will in your mundane actions so the non-magical can be used to help you achieve your goals too. Do not be too afraid because often the greatest teacher in occultism is boldness: to use this magick here and really give the magick a good solid try. You need to lose any fear of magick straight away, and that takes practice. Magick is not just about a philosophical brain exercise it is more than that, it is the exploration of a strange and wonderful world and in time you will come to accept that the strange and unusual world you are exploring is this one. It is too easy for humanity to think of the world as being minus wonder and yet this isn't true at all, the world is full of wonder it is just often, we must seek the wonder rather than expect it to come to us.

Chapter 4 Love

Love isn't all you need after all food, drink and shelter are important too. However, I feel we do need love of some type and be that romantic love or the love a mother has for her daughter it is necessary. I want to help you and so I offer magick to attract love: so that it will flow to you.

Three King Mages magick to attract love

Janus the powerful Roman god, he with two faces and while one looks towards the future another looks towards the past. Janus you control doorways and so I ask that you open the doorway that leads to the Three King Mages, the men of wisdom, Balthazar, Gaspar and Melchior, they who brought the three presents of gold, frankincense and myrrh. Janus open the doorway: Janus does open the doorway it is opening it is open here and now. I summon through the doorway the King Mage Balthazar, he who carried gold. Balthazar, King Mage

step through the doorway and be here with me: Balthazar does step through the doorway and is here with me. King Mage Gaspar you who carried the gift of frankincense, I ask that you come through the doorway and be here with me, Gaspar the wise man, I ask that you come to this place: Gaspar does step through the doorway and is here with me. King Mage Melchior he who carried myrrh, I ask that you step through the doorway and be here with me: Melchior does step through the doorway and is here with me. Balthazar, I ask that you attract love to me. Gaspar, I ask that you attract love to me. Melchior, I ask that you attract love to me. Balthazar agrees to help and departs back through the doorway. Gaspar agrees to help and departs back through the doorway. Melchior agrees to help and departs back through the doorway. Janus the powerful Roman god, he with two faces and while one looks towards the future another looks towards the past. Janus you control doorways and so I ask that you shut the doorway, Janus close the doorway: Janus does shut the doorway it is closing it is closed here and now. So it is and will be.

26

Sex is different from love because just as love can easily exist without sex, so sex can exist without even the slightest amount of love. This magick will get sex to flow to you always. I understand that magick such as this will make your life more pleasurable and so here it is for you to use.

Three King Mages magick to attract sex

Janus the powerful Roman god, he with two faces and while one looks towards the future another looks towards the past. Janus you control doorways and so I ask that you open the doorway that leads to the Three King Mages, the men of wisdom, Balthazar, Gaspar and Melchior, they who brought the three presents of gold, frankincense and myrrh. Janus open the doorway: Janus does open the doorway it is opening it is open here and now. I summon through the doorway the King Mage Balthazar, he who carried gold. Balthazar, King Mage step through the doorway and be here with me: Balthazar does step through the doorway and is here with me. King Mage Gaspar you

who carried the gift of frankincense, I ask that you come through the doorway and be here with me, Gaspar the wise man, I ask that you come to this place: Gaspar does step through the doorway and is here with me. King Mage Melchior he who carried myrrh, I ask that you step through the doorway and be here with me: Melchior does step through the doorway and is here with me. Balthazar, I ask that you attract sex to me. Gaspar, I ask that you attract sex to me. Melchior, I ask that you attract sex to me. Balthazar agrees to help and departs back through the doorway. Gaspar agrees to help and departs back through the doorway. Melchior agrees to help and departs back through the doorway. Janus the powerful Roman god, he with two faces and while one looks towards the future another looks towards the past. Janus you control doorways and so I ask that you shut the doorway, Janus close the doorway: Janus does shut the doorway it is closing it is closed here and now. So it is and will be.

If you are one of those people who desires to have many lovers then please do work this next magick so that it may help you. I understand that for some people lots of lovers isn't something they desire. But we are all of us individuals and so I offer magick to help you; and here it is.

Three King Mages magick to have many lovers

Janus the powerful Roman god, he with two faces and while one looks towards the future another looks towards the past. Janus you control doorways and so I ask that you open the doorway that leads to the Three King Mages, the men of wisdom, Balthazar, Gaspar and Melchior, they who brought the three presents of gold, frankincense and myrrh. Janus open the doorway: Janus does open the doorway it is opening it is open here and now. I summon through the doorway the King Mage Balthazar, he who carried gold. Balthazar, King Mage step through the doorway and be here with me: Balthazar does step through the doorway and is here with me. King Mage Gaspar you

who carried the gift of frankincense, I ask that you come through the doorway and be here with me, Gaspar the wise man, I ask that you come to this place: Gaspar does step through the doorway and is here with me. King Mage Melchior he who carried myrrh, I ask that you step through the doorway and be here with me: Melchior does step through the doorway and is here with me. Balthazar, I ask that you give me many lovers. Gaspar, I ask that you give me many lovers. Melchior, I ask that you give me many lovers. Balthazar agrees to help and departs back through the doorway. Gaspar agrees to help and departs back through the doorway. Melchior agrees to help and departs back through the doorway. Janus the powerful Roman god, he with two faces and while one looks towards the future another looks towards the past. Janus you control doorways and so I ask that you shut the doorway, Janus close the doorway: Janus does shut the doorway it is closing it is closed here and now. So it is and will be.

I will now show you magick that will be aimed at a specific person: someone of your choosing. I understand that magick such as this may cause long term relationships even, because after a while it becomes routine. However, someone may come for the magick but they will stay because of you. Work this magick with a strong will so that it will work.

Three King Mages magick for the love of a chosen person

Janus the powerful Roman god, he with two faces and while one looks towards the future another looks towards the past. Janus you control doorways and so I ask that you open the doorway that leads to the Three King Mages, the men of wisdom, Balthazar, Gaspar and Melchior, they who brought the three presents of gold, frankincense and myrrh. Janus open the doorway: Janus does open the doorway it is opening it is open here and now. I summon through the doorway the King Mage Balthazar, he who carried gold. Balthazar, King Mage step through the doorway and be here with me: Balthazar does step through the doorway and is here with me. King Mage Gaspar you who carried the gift of frankincense, I ask that you come through the doorway and be here with me, Gaspar the wise man, I ask that you come to this place: Gaspar does step through the doorway and is here with me. King Mage Melchior he who carried myrrh, I ask that you step through the doorway and be here with me: Melchior does step through the doorway and is here with me. Balthazar, I ask that you make state name of chosen person love me. Gaspar, I ask that you make state name of chosen person love me. Melchior, I ask that you make state name of chosen person love me. Balthazar agrees to help and departs back through the doorway. Gaspar agrees to help and departs back through the doorway. Melchior agrees to help and departs back through the doorway. Janus the powerful Roman god, he with two faces and while one looks towards the future another looks towards the past. Janus you control doorways and so I ask that you shut the doorway, Janus close the doorway: Janus does shut the doorway it is closing it is closed here and now. So it is and will be.

32

You now understand that even love and sex are not outside the confines of this magick. I understand that this may be shocking because many people have the opinion that love is beyond magick somehow when it is not really at all. It is the most terrible thing to be loveless if one feels a need for love within them. Have love, work the magick in this chapter again and again; it will help you.

Chapter 5 Money

I now present some magick to attract money to you. Unless we are monks, money is important and we must live in the world and know that without this one thing we would surely die. We have built a world where no money equals death. I suppose this is why people die over money or a lack of it: this is both sad, monstrous and tragic simultaneously.

Three King Mages magick to attract money

Janus the powerful Roman god, he with two faces and while one looks towards the future another looks towards the past. Janus you control doorways and so I ask that you open the doorway that leads to the Three King Mages, the men of wisdom, Balthazar, Gaspar and Melchior, they who brought the three presents of gold, frankincense and myrrh. Janus open the doorway: Janus does open the doorway it is opening it is open here and now. I summon through the doorway

the King Mage Balthazar, he who carried gold. Balthazar, King Mage step through the doorway and be here with me: Balthazar does step through the doorway and is here with me. King Mage Gaspar you who carried the gift of frankincense, I ask that you come through the doorway and be here with me, Gaspar the wise man, I ask that you come to this place: Gaspar does step through the doorway and is here with me. King Mage Melchior he who carried myrrh, I ask that you step through the doorway and be here with me: Melchior does step through the doorway and is here with me. Balthazar, I ask that you attract money to me. Gaspar, I ask that you attract money to me. Melchior, I ask that you attract money to me. Balthazar agrees to help and departs back through the doorway. Gaspar agrees to help and departs back through the doorway. Melchior agrees to help and departs back through the doorway. Janus the powerful Roman god, he with two faces and while one looks towards the future another looks towards the past. Janus you control doorways and so I ask that

you shut the doorway, Janus close the doorway: Janus does shut the doorway it is closing it is closed here and now. So it is and will be.

Why not have enough money and assets to be considered rich. I feel that being rich has few disadvantages whereas being poor has many more. I understand that a lot of wealth sometimes leads people to do things that are inadvisable and normally out of reach. In fact, any mistakes you make because you are rich is not the fault of the money it is your fault. The next magick follows now.

Three King Mages magick to be rich

Janus the powerful Roman god, he with two faces and while one looks towards the future another looks towards the past. Janus you control doorways and so I ask that you open the doorway that leads to the Three King Mages, the men of wisdom, Balthazar, Gaspar and Melchior, they who brought the three presents of gold, frankincense and myrrh. Janus open the doorway: Janus does open the doorway it is opening it is open here and now. I summon through the doorway

the King Mage Balthazar, he who carried gold. Balthazar, King Mage step through the doorway and be here with me: Balthazar does step through the doorway and is here with me. King Mage Gaspar you who carried the gift of frankincense, I ask that you come through the doorway and be here with me, Gaspar the wise man, I ask that you come to this place: Gaspar does step through the doorway and is here with me. King Mage Melchior he who carried myrrh, I ask that you step through the doorway and be here with me: Melchior does step through the doorway and is here with me. Balthazar, I ask that you make me rich. Gaspar, I ask that you make me rich. Melchior, I ask that you make me rich. Balthazar agrees to help and departs back through the doorway. Gaspar agrees to help and departs back through the doorway. Melchior agrees to help and departs back through the doorway. Janus the powerful Roman god, he with two faces and while one looks towards the future another looks towards the past. Janus you control doorways and so I ask that you shut the doorway, Janus close the doorway: Janus does shut the doorway it is closing it is closed here and now. So it is and will be.

The super-rich have wealth in a level all of their own. These people may live opulently and know that they are only touching the top of the money they have because it is so vast that their problem would be from stopping money from piling up. To be super-rich isn't easy to achieve simply through magick and so do think on what plans you can make so that your magick has a road to get the assets to you so you can be super-rich.

Three King Mages magick to be super-rich

Janus the powerful Roman god, he with two faces and while one looks towards the future another looks towards the past. Janus you control doorways and so I ask that you open the doorway that leads to the Three King Mages, the men of wisdom, Balthazar, Gaspar and Melchior, they who brought the three presents of gold, frankincense and myrrh. Janus open the doorway: Janus does open the doorway it is opening it is open here and now. I summon through the doorway the King Mage Balthazar, he who carried gold. Balthazar, King Mage step through the doorway and be here with me: Balthazar does step through the doorway and is here with me. King Mage Gaspar you who carried the gift of frankincense, I ask that you come through the doorway and be here with me, Gaspar the wise man, I ask that you come to this place: Gaspar does step through the doorway and is here with me. King Mage Melchior he who carried myrrh, I ask that you step through the doorway and be here with me: Melchior does step through the doorway and is here with me. Balthazar, I ask that you make me super-rich. Gaspar, I ask that you make me super-rich. Melchior, I ask that you make me super-rich. Balthazar agrees to help and departs back through the doorway. Gaspar agrees to help and departs back through the doorway. Melchior agrees to help and departs back through the doorway. Janus the powerful Roman god, he with two faces and while one looks towards the future another looks towards the past. Janus you control doorways and so I ask that

39

you shut the doorway, Janus close the doorway: Janus does shut the doorway it is closing it is closed here and now. So it is and will be.

Money is as much attached to real magick as anything else. The only trouble with money is that when one gains someone else loses: the rich make the poor and the poor make the rich. However, I talk of rich and poor as terms for people of wealth above or below a certain level. In fact, what the money of the poor buys them also comes down to design and progress because capitalism has made many things much less expensive than they formerly were. I feel that this is the state of richness versus the state of abundance: a man or woman with abundance may have everything you could desire and still not be rich because it is simply that capitalism has started to make these luxuries on a larger scale: making them cheaper. But here I have concentrated on money because with money you can get almost anything at all. Money is a way of storing power and is a medium of exchange; hence the reason why it can be exchanged for almost anything. I also think it good to mention that we have no choice in desiring money: at least to the sane mind: because we are not living in a monastery where everything we need is provided, we live in a place where things must be provided by us: bought using money. A person without food you would think would be in a situation worse than a person without money but it is not the case.

Chapter 6 Attacking

The fact is everyone has to attack at some point in time. Sometimes the best form of defense is attack: some one injured or dead cannot attack you: it would be difficult anyway. This next magick allows you to attack someone of your choosing through the use of magick alone. The advantage of this is that it is legal almost everywhere and can be done easily. In fact, occult assassinations have been done this way with great success: I am not actually saying I did them but you may draw your own conclusion if you desire.

Three King Mages magick to attack a chosen person

Janus the powerful Roman god, he with two faces and while one looks towards the future another looks towards the past. Janus you control doorways and so I ask that you open the doorway that leads to the Three King Mages, the men of wisdom, Balthazar, Gaspar and Melchior, they who brought the three presents of gold, frankincense and myrrh. Janus open the doorway: Janus does open the doorway it is opening it is open here and now. I summon through the doorway the King Mage Balthazar, he who carried gold. Balthazar, King Mage step through the doorway and be here with me: Balthazar does step through the doorway and is here with me. King Mage Gaspar you who carried the gift of frankincense, I ask that you come through the doorway and be here with me, Gaspar the wise man, I ask that you come to this place: Gaspar does step through the doorway and is here with me. King Mage Melchior he who carried myrrh, I ask that you step through the doorway and be here with me: Melchior does step through the doorway and is here with me. Balthazar, I ask that you attack state name of chosen person. Gaspar, I ask that you attack state name of chosen person. Melchior, I ask that you attack state name of chosen person. Balthazar agrees to help and departs back through the doorway. Gaspar agrees to help and departs back through the doorway. Melchior agrees to help and departs back through the doorway. Janus the powerful Roman god, he with two faces and while one looks towards the future another looks towards the past. Janus you control doorways and so I ask that you shut the doorway, Janus close the doorway: Janus does shut the doorway it is closing it is closed here and now. So it is and will be.

Here is some magick to attack an organization of your choosing. To work this magick is easy and shows how versatile the three King Mages are. You may not need this magick right now but you can have it working for you simply by performing this magick as follows.

Three King Mages magick to attack a chosen organization

Janus the powerful Roman god, he with two faces and while one looks towards the future another looks towards the past. Janus you control doorways and so I ask that you open the doorway that leads to the Three King Mages, the men of wisdom, Balthazar, Gaspar and Melchior, they who brought the three presents of gold, frankincense and myrrh. Janus open the doorway: Janus does open the doorway it is opening it is open here and now. I summon through the doorway

44

the King Mage Balthazar, he who carried gold. Balthazar, King Mage step through the doorway and be here with me: Balthazar does step through the doorway and is here with me. King Mage Gaspar you who carried the gift of frankincense, I ask that you come through the doorway and be here with me, Gaspar the wise man, I ask that you come to this place: Gaspar does step through the doorway and is here with me. King Mage Melchior he who carried myrrh, I ask that you step through the doorway and be here with me: Melchior does step through the doorway and is here with me. Balthazar, I ask that you attack the organization named state name of chosen organization. Gaspar, I ask that you attack the organization named state name of chosen organization. Melchior, I ask that you attack the organization named state name of chosen organization. Balthazar agrees to help and departs back through the doorway. Gaspar agrees to help and departs back through the doorway. Melchior agrees to help and departs back through the doorway. Janus the powerful Roman god, he with two faces and while one looks towards the future another looks towards the past. Janus you control doorways and so I ask that you shut the doorway, Janus close the doorway: Janus does shut the doorway it is closing it is closed here and now. So it is and will be.

We all have enemies and to my mind we should attack our enemies. I understand that to many people, the act of attacking enemies may seem alluring: and it should: but this magick adds one great addition you need not know who they are for this magick to work: you only need enemies. Perform this magick as follows.

Three King Mages magick to attack all enemies

Janus the powerful Roman god, he with two faces and while one looks towards the future another looks towards the past. Janus you control doorways and so I ask that you open the doorway that leads to the Three King Mages, the men of wisdom, Balthazar, Gaspar and Melchior, they who brought the three presents of gold, frankincense and myrrh. Janus open the doorway: Janus does open the doorway it is opening it is open here and now. I summon through the doorway

the King Mage Balthazar, he who carried gold. Balthazar, King Mage step through the doorway and be here with me: Balthazar does step through the doorway and is here with me. King Mage Gaspar you who carried the gift of frankincense, I ask that you come through the doorway and be here with me, Gaspar the wise man, I ask that you come to this place: Gaspar does step through the doorway and is here with me. King Mage Melchior he who carried myrrh, I ask that you step through the doorway and be here with me: Melchior does step through the doorway and is here with me. Balthazar, I ask that you attack all my enemies. Gaspar, I ask that you attack all my enemies. Melchior, I ask that you attack all my enemies. Balthazar agrees to help and departs back through the doorway. Gaspar agrees to help and departs back through the doorway. Melchior agrees to help and departs back through the doorway. Janus the powerful Roman god, he with two faces and while one looks towards the future another looks towards the past. Janus you control doorways and so I ask that

you shut the doorway, Janus close the doorway: Janus does shut the doorway it is closing it is closed here and now. So it is and will be.

I will now teach you how to attack people using a location instead of a name. This means that it will attack everyone at that location without prejudice: it will attack the old among the young, the innocent along with the guilty: however, there are times when this is the magick that is required.

Three King Mages magick to attack everyone at a chosen location or address

Janus the powerful Roman god, he with two faces and while one looks towards the future another looks towards the past. Janus you control doorways and so I ask that you open the doorway that leads to the Three King Mages, the men of wisdom, Balthazar, Gaspar and Melchior, they who brought the three presents of gold, frankincense and myrrh. Janus open the doorway: Janus does open the doorway it is opening it is open here and now. I summon through the doorway

48

the King Mage Balthazar, he who carried gold. Balthazar, King Mage step through the doorway and be here with me: Balthazar does step through the doorway and is here with me. King Mage Gaspar you who carried the gift of frankincense, I ask that you come through the doorway and be here with me, Gaspar the wise man, I ask that you come to this place: Gaspar does step through the doorway and is here with me. King Mage Melchior he who carried myrrh, I ask that you step through the doorway and be here with me: Melchior does step through the doorway and is here with me. Balthazar, I ask that you attack everyone at state name of chosen address or location. Gaspar, I ask that you attack everyone at state name of chosen address or location. Melchior, I ask that you attack everyone at state name of chosen address or location. Balthazar agrees to help and departs back through the doorway. Gaspar agrees to help and departs back through the doorway. Melchior agrees to help and departs back through the doorway. Janus the powerful Roman god, he with two faces and while one looks towards the future another looks towards the past. Janus

49

you control doorways and so I ask that you shut the doorway, Janus close the doorway: Janus does shut the doorway it is closing it is closed here and now. So it is and will be.

I think it important to congratulate you for working your way through the book this far because by this point your practical applicable knowledge has increased greatly. The truth is that learning magick is like learning to swim, it cannot be done on dry land so make sure you get wet in the pool of magick by working some of the magick that is here.

Chapter 7 Success

This chapter is devoted to success: in all its types and variations.

However, I have chosen to begin with general success: that success

that isn't for one particular type and this magick is easy to use and

here it is: will this magick to work so that it shall.

Three King Mages magick for general success

Janus the powerful Roman god, he with two faces and while one

looks towards the future another looks towards the past. Janus you

control doorways and so I ask that you open the doorway that leads

to the Three King Mages, the men of wisdom, Balthazar, Gaspar and

Melchior, they who brought the three presents of gold, frankincense

and myrrh. Janus open the doorway: Janus does open the doorway it

is opening it is open here and now. I summon through the doorway

the King Mage Balthazar, he who carried gold. Balthazar, King Mage

step through the doorway and be here with me: Balthazar does step through the doorway and is here with me. King Mage Gaspar you who carried the gift of frankincense, I ask that you come through the doorway and be here with me, Gaspar the wise man, I ask that you come to this place: Gaspar does step through the doorway and is here with me. King Mage Melchior he who carried myrrh, I ask that you step through the doorway and be here with me: Melchior does step through the doorway and is here with me. Balthazar, I ask that you make me successful. Gaspar, I ask that you make me successful. Melchior, I ask that you make me successful. Balthazar agrees to help and departs back through the doorway. Gaspar agrees to help and departs back through the doorway. Melchior agrees to help and departs back through the doorway. Janus the powerful Roman god, he with two faces and while one looks towards the future another looks towards the past. Janus you control doorways and so I ask that you shut the doorway, Janus close the doorway: Janus does shut the doorway it is closing it is closed here and now. So it is and will be.

Many people desire career success above any type and yet from the idea of this it would seem illogical. However, to some people their work is of such importance that they really must do the best they can and magick can help you achieve this. All you need do is to say these words while intending magick to be worked.

Three King Mages magick for career success

Janus the powerful Roman god, he with two faces and while one looks towards the future another looks towards the past. Janus you control doorways and so I ask that you open the doorway that leads to the Three King Mages, the men of wisdom, Balthazar, Gaspar and Melchior, they who brought the three presents of gold, frankincense and myrrh. Janus open the doorway: Janus does open the doorway it is opening it is open here and now. I summon through the doorway the King Mage Balthazar, he who carried gold. Balthazar, King Mage step through the doorway and be here with me: Balthazar does step through the doorway and is here with me. King Mage Gaspar you

who carried the gift of frankincense, I ask that you come through the doorway and be here with me, Gaspar the wise man, I ask that you come to this place: Gaspar does step through the doorway and is here with me. King Mage Melchior he who carried myrrh, I ask that you step through the doorway and be here with me: Melchior does step through the doorway and is here with me. Balthazar, I ask that you give me career successful. Gaspar, I ask that you give me career successful. Melchior, I ask that you give me career successful. Balthazar agrees to help and departs back through the doorway. Gaspar agrees to help and departs back through the doorway. Melchior agrees to help and departs back through the doorway. Janus the powerful Roman god, he with two faces and while one looks towards the future another looks towards the past. Janus you control doorways and so I ask that you shut the doorway, Janus close the doorway: Janus does shut the doorway it is closing it is closed here and now. So it is and will be.

Many people desire financial success and so I have here some magick to assist you: so that you may achieve this. This magick is not too difficult and is something important to us. I do think you should work strongly on working this magick because it will enhance your life to a large degree.

Three King Mages magick for financial success

Janus the powerful Roman god, he with two faces and while one looks towards the future another looks towards the past. Janus you control doorways and so I ask that you open the doorway that leads to the Three King Mages, the men of wisdom, Balthazar, Gaspar and Melchior, they who brought the three presents of gold, frankincense and myrrh. Janus open the doorway: Janus does open the doorway it is opening it is open here and now. I summon through the doorway the King Mage Balthazar, he who carried gold. Balthazar, King Mage step through the doorway and be here with me: Balthazar does step through the doorway and is here with me. King Mage Gaspar you

who carried the gift of frankincense, I ask that you come through the doorway and be here with me, Gaspar the wise man, I ask that you come to this place: Gaspar does step through the doorway and is here with me. King Mage Melchior he who carried myrrh, I ask that you step through the doorway and be here with me: Melchior does step through the doorway and is here with me. Balthazar, I ask that you give me financial success. Gaspar, I ask that you give me financial success. Melchior, I ask that you give me financial success. Balthazar agrees to help and departs back through the doorway. Gaspar agrees to help and departs back through the doorway. Melchior agrees to help and departs back through the doorway. Janus the powerful Roman god, he with two faces and while one looks towards the future another looks towards the past. Janus you control doorways and so I ask that you shut the doorway, Janus close the doorway: Janus does shut the doorway it is closing it is closed here and now. So it is and will be.

I feel that this book is an exploration for the reader because you are going through land which to you is unchartered and opens your mind to other possibilities. You have the right to the advantages of this magick because it was you who learnt what is here and performed the magick. The truth is that magick being a power that occultists use is fair in a world where nothing else is because the people using it had to learn how.

Chapter 8 Fame

This chapter concentrates on fame and its different types. There are many types of fame and a person may find they are famous within a particular subject or genre or by geographical area: some are famous everywhere in all ways. To have many fans work this next magick: it will help you get just that.

Three King Mages magick for have many fans

Janus the powerful Roman god, he with two faces and while one looks towards the future another looks towards the past. Janus you control doorways and so I ask that you open the doorway that leads to the Three King Mages, the men of wisdom, Balthazar, Gaspar and Melchior, they who brought the three presents of gold, frankincense and myrrh. Janus open the doorway: Janus does open the doorway it is opening it is open here and now. I summon through the doorway the King Mage Balthazar, he who carried gold. Balthazar, King Mage

step through the doorway and be here with me: Balthazar does step through the doorway and is here with me. King Mage Gaspar you who carried the gift of frankincense, I ask that you come through the doorway and be here with me, Gaspar the wise man, I ask that you come to this place: Gaspar does step through the doorway and is here with me. King Mage Melchior he who carried myrrh, I ask that you step through the doorway and be here with me: Melchior does step through the doorway and is here with me. Balthazar, I ask that you give me many fans. Gaspar, I ask that you give me many fans. Melchior, I ask that you give me many fans. Balthazar agrees to help and departs back through the doorway. Gaspar agrees to help and departs back through the doorway. Melchior agrees to help and departs back through the doorway. Janus the powerful Roman god, he with two faces and while one looks towards the future another looks towards the past. Janus you control doorways and so I ask that you shut the doorway, Janus close the doorway: Janus does shut the doorway it is closing it is closed here and now. So it is and will be.

One level of fame is to be well known and there is no more to it than that. But like all the magick here you must will it to work as you perform the magick. In fact, some people become well known simply through the act of being noticeable. In smaller locations simply the wearing of a trilby hat can be enough to render one with this first degree of fame. Magick to assist you follows.

Three King Mages magick to be well known

Janus the powerful Roman god, he with two faces and while one looks towards the future another looks towards the past. Janus you control doorways and so I ask that you open the doorway that leads to the Three King Mages, the men of wisdom, Balthazar, Gaspar and Melchior, they who brought the three presents of gold, frankincense and myrrh. Janus open the doorway: Janus does open the doorway it is opening it is open here and now. I summon through the doorway the King Mage Balthazar, he who carried gold. Balthazar, King Mage step through the doorway and be here with me: Balthazar does step through the doorway and is here with me. King Mage Gaspar you who carried the gift of frankincense, I ask that you come through the doorway and be here with me, Gaspar the wise man, I ask that you come to this place: Gaspar does step through the doorway and is here with me. King Mage Melchior he who carried myrrh, I ask that you step through the doorway and be here with me: Melchior does step through the doorway and is here with me. Balthazar, I ask that you make me well known. Gaspar, I ask that you make me well known. Melchior, I ask that you make me well known. Balthazar agrees to help and departs back through the doorway. Gaspar agrees to help and departs back through the doorway. Melchior agrees to help and departs back through the doorway. Janus the powerful Roman god, he with two faces and while one looks towards the future another looks towards the past. Janus you control doorways and so I ask that you shut the doorway, Janus close the doorway: Janus does shut the doorway it is closing it is closed here and now. So it is and will be.

One type of fame that used to be easy to get is to be a local celebrity: the area of a local celebrity varies on the size of your country and the area you live. In fact, in some countries a local celebrity may be the size of the country I live in: Britain: whereas for some much smaller. However, being a local celebrity is something that is worthwhile and you can have more than one sort of fame, so if you really want to be famous work all the magick in this chapter.

Three King Mages magick to be a local celebrity

Janus the powerful Roman god, he with two faces and while one looks towards the future another looks towards the past. Janus you control doorways and so I ask that you open the doorway that leads to the Three King Mages, the men of wisdom, Balthazar, Gaspar and Melchior, they who brought the three presents of gold, frankincense and myrrh. Janus open the doorway: Janus does open the doorway it is opening it is open here and now. I summon through the doorway the King Mage Balthazar, he who carried gold. Balthazar, King Mage

step through the doorway and be here with me: Balthazar does step through the doorway and is here with me. King Mage Gaspar you who carried the gift of frankincense, I ask that you come through the doorway and be here with me, Gaspar the wise man, I ask that you come to this place: Gaspar does step through the doorway and is here with me. King Mage Melchior he who carried myrrh, I ask that you step through the doorway and be here with me: Melchior does step through the doorway and is here with me. Balthazar, I ask that you make me a local celebrity. Gaspar, I ask that you make me a local celebrity. Melchior, I ask that you make me a local celebrity. Balthazar agrees to help and departs back through the doorway. Gaspar agrees to help and departs back through the doorway. Melchior agrees to help and departs back through the doorway. Janus the powerful Roman god, he with two faces and while one looks towards the future another looks towards the past. Janus you control doorways and so I ask that you shut the doorway, Janus close the doorway: Janus does shut the doorway it is closing it is closed here and now. So it is and will be.

Worldwide fame means just that, that you are known all over the world. To gain this there is very likely to be things you need to do. In fact, at one time being famous for doing something was the main route whereas now some people are famous for nothing at all other than trying to sell their celebrity perfumes. However, do use this magick so that this important type of magick can be yours.

Three King Mages magick for worldwide fame

Janus the powerful Roman god, he with two faces and while one looks towards the future another looks towards the past. Janus you control doorways and so I ask that you open the doorway that leads to the Three King Mages, the men of wisdom, Balthazar, Gaspar and Melchior, they who brought the three presents of gold, frankincense and myrrh. Janus open the doorway: Janus does open the doorway it is opening it is open here and now. I summon through the doorway

the King Mage Balthazar, he who carried gold. Balthazar, King Mage step through the doorway and be here with me: Balthazar does step through the doorway and is here with me. King Mage Gaspar you who carried the gift of frankincense, I ask that you come through the doorway and be here with me, Gaspar the wise man, I ask that you come to this place: Gaspar does step through the doorway and is here with me. King Mage Melchior he who carried myrrh, I ask that you step through the doorway and be here with me: Melchior does step through the doorway and is here with me. Balthazar, I ask that you make me famous worldwide. Gaspar, I ask that you make me famous worldwide. Melchior, I ask that you make me famous worldwide. Balthazar agrees to help and departs back through the doorway. Gaspar agrees to help and departs back through the doorway. Melchior agrees to help and departs back through the doorway. Janus the powerful Roman god, he with two faces and while one looks towards the future another looks towards the past. Janus you control doorways and so I ask that you shut the doorway, Janus close the doorway: Janus does shut the doorway it is closing it is closed here and now. So it is and will be.

You have now come to the end of the book and you have learnt a lot. It would be true to say that you have now a great overview of this magick and a potent repertoire of magick. I feel that occultism is something we all should know about and use when appropriate. But what is more important to me is freedom of expression and freedom from slavery and torture. I say this because when people have no power at all they are easy meat for the torturers of the world and in some locations may even become enslaved. I wish to free the slaves: preventing them is better in many ways and so I write this book knowing it will empower you and make one less person capable of being enslaved. Let the magick give freedom to all. Freedom to you, freedom to me, freedom for all.

www.ingramcontent.com/pod-product-compliance
Lightning Source LLC
La Vergne TN
LVHW021544080426
835509LV00019B/2836